Bodmin Gaol

Cornwall

by

Alan Brunton

Illustrations by

Ann Brightmore-Armour

ACKNOWLEDGEMENTS

Hazel James and Fred Hellen } for their help
Maureen Tooze and Bodmin Museum } and information
Bodmin Library
Terry Gilhooly - present owner of Bodmin Gaol
Kenneth Major and his publication "Animal Powered Machines".
Joan Carr for typing the original manuscript.
My wife Fran for acting as chauffeur.
And anyone not mentioned above who freely gave their time and assistance helping me gather information for this book.

"Whilst all care has been exercised, the author cannot accept responsibility for any inaccuracies. Whilst undertaking research for this book I on occasion found variations on some of the gaol's history. I have recorded those I consider to be most likely correct."

Alan Brunton.

ISBN 0 9519027 0 9.

First published 1992 by Orchard Publications, Devon.
This edition published 1995 by Terry Gilhooly, Bodmin Gaol.
Further copies of this book can be obtained from
Bodmin Gaol, Berrycombe Road, Bodmin, Cornwall PL31 2NR
Telephone 01208 76292.
Printed by Nationwide Print, St. Austell, Cornwall (01726 72548).

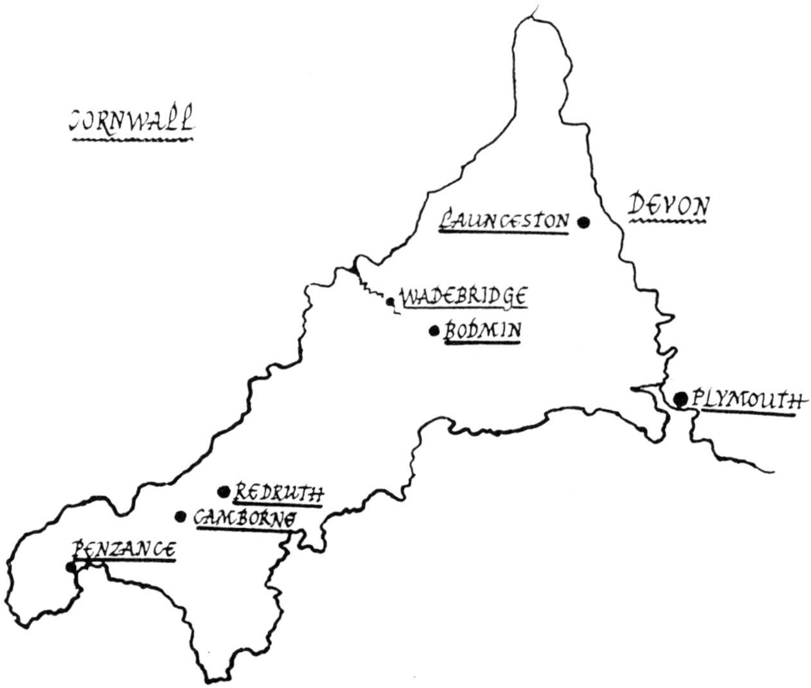

BODMIN GAOL

The first Bodmin gaol was built in 1779 on the same site as the present gaol, which was completed in 1860. Prior to this the Cornwall County Gaol was housed in Launceston Castle. Part of the castle continued as a prison, on a much reduced scale, until 1829, when it was finally closed.

In the mid-1770's local Justices of the Peace made representations to government as to the need for a new gaol in Cornwall. Conditions in Launceston were so bad that several JPs could not bring themselves to commit convicted persons to such a deplorable place. Launceston was also felt to be too remote to the rest of Cornwall, making the transportation of prisoners time-consuming and therefore extremely costly. Bodmin was far more central.

The first and subsequent gaols were built to high standards and, although some of the treatment handed out to the inmates was at times severely harsh, general living conditions were better than some of them would have enjoyed outside.

Launceston Castle showing old County gaol in foreground. The prison closed in 1829 and was demolished in 1840. The grounds were then landscaped and used as a public park. Although remaining in the ownership of the Duchy of Cornwall the castle has been maintained by English Heritage since 1984. It is open to the public and well worth visiting.

1779 - 1860

Very little, if indeed any, of the original prison remains today, although it is thought highly probable that some of the original building materials were incorporated in the second prison.

During the period 1770-1774 John Howard, later known for his penal reform recommendations, was commissioned by Parliament to tour the prisons of Europe on a 'fact finding' mission. Many of his subsequent proposals were employed in the building and management of Bodmin gaol.

The Government provided the £5,000 needed to build the prison, and Bodmin Corporation provided the site known then as Burcom. The gaol stands today alongside Berrycombe Road - Berrycombe shortened to Burcom by the local folk. The architect was a Mr. Jones of Exeter, building supervisor John Call, and James Chapple was works foreman. On completion and occupation of the gaol James Chapple was appointed the prison's first governor, a post he held for nearly fifty years. One must assume he was either a very young works foreman or a rather old governor! He died in 1827.

Men and women were housed in the same prison building, though separated by internal walls. It was built to house one hundred prisoners. Prison records show the inmate population to be as follows:

1779	-	13
1782	-	26
1787	-	47
1814	-	39
1831	-	182
1838	-	117
1840	-	155 (including 38 women)

It can be seen from these figures that within fifty years of receiving its first prisoner the gaol was already becoming overcrowded. In the early nineteenth century Cornwall's population rose from 200,000 in 1805 to around 303,000 in 1830. The increase in population was due to better employment opportunities in industry and improvements in the roads system. An increase in the crime rate followed, hence the gaol overcrowding.

The gaol contained a Debtor's Ward, self-explanatory, and a Bridewell. The Bridewell housed those found guilty of minor offences, although one must wonder what constituted a minor offence when in 1787 William Congdon was hung for stealing a watch, and in 1825 William Oxford suffered the same fate after being found guilty of setting fire to a corn stack.

Prisoners were allocated separate cells, though with the increase in custodial sentences this was not always possible. As mentioned earlier, Launceston Castle was still used to ease the overcrowding up until 1829. This party explains the vast increase in recorded numbers of prisoners in Bodmin in 1831. When it was declared that Launceston was to close its gaol, plans were drawn up to enlarge Bodmin, and between 1830-1847 building work was undertaken to ensure that considerably more than the original one hundred prisoners could be accommodated.

Each cell was approximately 8 feet by 6 feet, with maximum head room of 7 feet 6 inches. Inside would be a bedstead, straw for bedding, and two or three blankets. The debtors' and minor offenders' quarters were slightly larger. Cells were whitewashed frequently, washed once or twice weekly, and swept daily. All this work would have been carried out by the inmates. As recommended in John Howard's Reform Charter, all prisoners were expected to work. Those serving the longest sentences were often committed to hard labour, whilst others were given work in the gardens, wood sawing, shoemaking and marble stone polishing. Women prisoners were employed spinning and weaving and working in the prison laundry. The hardest work given to a prisoner in the hard labour category was to be put on the Treadwheel. A comprehensive chapter on the Treadwheel will be found later in this book. Several Treadwheels were used in the new prison, between 1860-1896. Many of the prisoners received a daily allowance for their labours. The debtors were allowed to keep most of their earnings, thereby enabling them to pay off their creditors, whilst some of the prisoners kept just one penny out of every six they earned. The rest was retained as a 'rent' towards their upkeep.

Amongst the prisoners were a large number of juveniles under sixteen years of age. They received limited education from the prison governor and his clerk who doubled as schoolmasters. Prison reforms were regularly being introduced and in 1854 admission to Bodmin gaol for juvenile offenders was abolished in favour of a Borstal-style correction centre elsewhere in Bodmin.

The prison housed two hospital rooms and a surgeon was always on call. Water was drawn from a local source and the wards contained two baths, stone troughs with running water and a boiler to provide hot water. Beneath these rooms were the condemned cells for those facing the ultimate punishment.

Prior to the gaol being built, and for a few years after, hangings were conducted on Bodmin Moor. It was not until 1802 that these were transferred to the prison. Records do not tell us clearly whether the hangings which took place between 1802-1816 were carried out on the moor or at the gaol. However, we do know that the site on the moor used for the hangings was donated in 1816 by Bodmin Town Council for the building of St. Lawrence's County Asylum.

The first recorded hanging was in 1785. Philip Randall aged twenty-seven, faced the gallows for burglary. Public hangings were meant as a deterrent but they came to be regarded as popular entertainment. A public hanging attracted vast crowds to Bodmin and meant good business for local tradesmen. Large crowds also drew many pick-pockets and members of the criminal element. For some of them, their stay in Bodmin turned out to be longer than originally intended. Indeed, some of the local tradesmen must have become quite prosperous for there were a further nineteen public hangings between 1785-1798. Spectators really had value for money on March 31st, 1791. Michael Taylor aged twenty-two,

Public hangings were intended as deterrents but came to be regarded as popular entertainment

John Dash aged twenty-three, and James Symons aged twenty-five, all felt the rope around their necks on this day. Hangings at the old gaol took place at twelve noon. The bodies were left suspended for an hour and one minute and, when cut down, were often carried away to local doctors' surgeries for dissection and for the benefit of medical science.

After 1816 public hangings took place just outside the main South wall. The chaplain, the hangman and condemned man would exit the prison through a small door in the wall onto the gallows platform. The watching crowds amassed in the fields and on the opposite hill to obtain a fine view of all proceedings.

During the 1830's the railway line was completed between Bodmin and Wadebridge - one of the first railway lines in the country. This line ran parallel with the prison South wall and coal wagons were able to unload directly into the prison coal depot. The coal was used in the gaol's boilers which served the hospital rooms and laundry. This railway line also enabled even larger crowds to attend the public hangings. People would journey to Wadebridge from Padstow, Camelford and surrounding districts and pack the trains to Bodmin; cheap day returns and no extra charge for the entertainment!

The last public hanging was that of John Doidge in 1862. This took place at the new time of eight o'clock in the morning. The executions of Selina Wadge in 1878 and William Bartlett in 1882 were conducted out of public view, and the prison hangings of Giovanni Valeri in 1901 and William Hampton in 1909 were carried out in the execution shed, a site not used previously, located in the north-east corner of the new gaol or, as one enters the main gate off Bodiniel Road, just inside to the right. When Bodmin gaol closed, hangings were transferred to Exeter prison.

At the turn of the nineteenth century there were over one hundred and sixty crimes carrying the death penalty. In 1823 Robert Peel, the Home Secretary, introduced an Act of Parliament known as Peel's Gaol Act which reduced this number considerably, thus by the time the new gaol was opened in 1860 and further reforms had been introduced, the death penalty applied for treason and murder only.

The gaol gave all prisoners religious instruction. In 1803 Reverend Morgan was appointed Chaplain and he was succeeded in 1821 by the Reverend Fayner. Prisoners attended chapel service daily. Women

prisoners were screened from the men, and those convicts awaiting the hangman sat in a separate pew.
James Chapple suffered ill-health in his later years as prison governor and John Bentham Everest, a serving officer on the convict ships in Chatham and Sheerness, was appointed the new governor.

Prison main entrance off Bodiniel Road. Now serves as visitors' entrance.

1860 - 1929

Two of John Howard's Penal Reform recommendations in 1774 were the separation of, and no contact between, prisoners, thus ensuring silence in the gaol at all times. Despite the expansion programme of the old gaol, overcrowding was still causing major problems and these recommendations were proving virtually impossible to maintain.

In 1855 the authorities granted £25,000 to be made available for the building of a new prison on the existing, but somewhat enlarged, site. Plans were issued and tenders for the building contract invited. Messrs. Goodyear and Son of Plymouth tendered £28,000. Although over budget, their's was the lowest and they were granted the work. During late 1869 and early 1870 the Royal Cornwall Gazette carried a series of articles on Bodmin Gaol. An extract taken from one of these articles puts the final cost as being "upwards of forty thousand pounds".

Thus the building of the present Bodmin Gaol commenced in 1857 and created much disruption to the day to day running of the existing gaol. However, benefits were also derived. Many of the prisoners were put to work quarrying granite from a local source. Mr. Fred Hellen, a Bodmin man whose father once owned the Chaplaincy and Governor's House after the gaol was sold at public auction, recalls his father telling him the granite was dug out of a quarry close to where Flaxmoor Terrace stands today. This quarry is known by locals as Cuckoo Quarry and has since been filled in with hardcore and surplus soil when a nearby housing estate was built. Although

Cuckoo Quarry. Over 20,000 tons of granite were quarried from this source towards the building of the new gaol.

this quarrying was another form of hard labour for the prisoners, some of them undoubtedly welcomed it. Better to be out in the fresh air than in a solitary cell oakum picking! Over twenty thousand tons of granite were quarried before the site was worked out and extra stone had to be purchased from outside sources. Building was completed and the gaol first occupied in February 1860.

Even as it stands today, having suffered much demolition during the last sixty years, one can appreciate the tremendous skill and workmanship that went into this building. We know labour resources were plentiful, but considering completion was within four years it was a magnificent piece of work by Messrs. Goodyear and Son. Prisons can never be described as attractive examples of period architecture, yet Bodmin's has a feel of superb craftsmanship about it. As the new gaol was constructed, the old one was pulled down. Around this time John Bentham Everest retired as prison governor to be succeeded by Captain Hugh Colville.

Governor's House and Chaplaincy. Now privately owned.

Delabole - 1860.
The slate quarry has been Delabole's life blood for hundreds of years.
The quarry is the largest man made hole in Europe, measuring over 500 feet deep and exceeding one mile in circumference. The complex is well worth visiting, offering viewing facilities, museum and craft shop.

The new gaol contained over two hundred cells, of which a quarter were for female use, eight punishment cells to the same ratio, and a condemned cell. It also housed a hospital block, administration offices, library, chapel, kitchens, laundry and workrooms. There was also a stabling block and a few staff quarters. The Governor's house and Chaplaincy were built outside the prison to the left of the main entrance. These are now privately owned and still so named.

Artist's impression of cell block interior.

The cells were larger than the old ones: 13 feet long, 7 feet wide and 9 feet high. The condemned cell was considerably larger. Some of the cells and condemned cell can be viewed today. The cell floors and gallery landings were of Delabole slate, a material much used throughout the prison. It was easy to clean and plentiful in supply, Delabole being only twenty miles away. When the prison was sold into private ownership in 1929 most of the slate was removed. A spiral stone staircase and stone/granite staircases led to the various prison floors. The slate landings were supported by steel girders, and wire netting was extended from gallery to gallery to prevent suicides. A similar design is used in some of our modern day prisons. A tuberculosis cell was also provided, tuberculosis being a disease prevalent in those days.

Gas burners for heating and lighting were provided in each cell but only used in the winter months. In the centre of each cell door at ground level was a trap door through which the prisoner's food was passed. There was an eye level spy hole covered by a moveable metal plate, through which the warder could view the cell interior. An original cell door with these examples is exhibited in the town's Museum. Also on view are further examples of the slate boards giving the cell number, prisoner's initials, date of confinement, offence committed, class of diet and work programme the prisoner was to receive, and date of sentence expiry. These boards were attached to the exterior of the cell door Prisoners were never referred to by name, only by their cell number.

Captain Hugh Colville's position as prison governor was taken over by a Mr. Stevens, who himself was succeeded in 1887 by Mr. Shenton. Having had just two governors during the previous eighty years Bodmin gaol had now seen a further three gentlemen occupy this position over the next twenty-seven years. With the building of more prisons it is probable the governors with experience were promoted to the new gaols.

Classes of prisoner and diet.

When entering the gaol at the commencement of their sentence prisoners were allocated a class. There were five classes, and the length and type of sentence determined which class they were placed in. The class also determined the diet each prisoner was to receive. Generally the longer the sentence the better the food. Prisoners serving longer sentences were often given hard labour, so, to ensure their capability for fulfilling hard labour their diet was improved. Whether this "class" system was adopted in 1860 is not really clear, but it was certainly in operation between 1870 - 1880.

Class 1 Prisoners serving 14 days or less.
Class 2 Exceeding 14 days up to one calendar month.
Class 3 Exceeding one month - up to two calendar months.
Class 4 Exceeding two calendar months.

Class 4B Hard labour sentences of two to six calendar months.
Class 5 Hard labour sentences in excess of six calendar months.

Three meals a day were served: breakfast, dinner and supper. The food was basic but reasonably wholesome. Bread and gruel constituted the main diet, with occasional supplements of dressed meat, potatoes and soup. The majority of inmates had only water to drink.

Prisoners in classes one and two were given only the bread and gruel, unless they were sentenced to spend part of their term doing hard labour. Soup would then have been added to their diet. Prisoners in classes three, four and five would have received the bread and a stronger gruel - gruel being a version of porridge, and various quantities of potatoes, soup and dressed meat.

The kitchens were well maintained and worked by "star" male prisoners. These were men of previous good character who would have been in employment before their confinement. All meals were consumed in the prisoners' cells. Female prisoners were given similar diets but not the same quantity in each meal. However, for those working in the laundry extra bread would have been supplied.

For the prisoners receiving medical attention, the diets would have been more flexible, in line with the surgeon's instructions. Records show for the year ending September 1874 the average weekly cost of food per prisoner was two shillings, one penny and three farthings - written 2s 13/4d: the value nowadays of ten and a half pence. It must be remembered that for many of the working class of this period their diet outside of gaol was probably little better than that of those in gaol.

Hard Labour

Hard labour was divided into two categories: first class and second class.

Hard labour first class:

The Treadwheel. An eight hour shift working four hours and resting four hours in alternate periods of fifteen minutes During the so called rest periods the prisoners would have been engaged in mat weaving, bag making, oakum picking, or any arduous task topical to prison requirements at the time.

Hard labour second class:
Oakum picking, mat and bag making, and again any heavy work to prison requirements - stone breaking, wood sawing, etc.

THE TREADWHEEL:
Also known as the treadmill as it was later adapted to grind corn for the prison population. The Treadwheel was first used in the old gaol in 1822. Its design was based on the one in use in Brixton gaol. A further thirteen prisons throughout the country introduced it during 1823. Without doubt it was the most severe form of hard labour. It is probable several wheels were used during the period 1822 - 1870. In 1869 records show that an additional £1,800 was spent at Bodmin in constructing a building housing a treadwheel and corn mill. This must have been the wheel capable of accommodating thirty-two men at a

The treadmill in Brixton prison from an illustrated paper of about 1830. The treadmill at Bodmin was much larger, capable of taking up to 32 men, each one partitioned from the other.

time. Some of the smaller wheels would have been dismantled. The speed of the wheel could be regulated but would normally be set to compel each man to take forty-five steps per minute. Several prisoners suffered hernias whilst working the wheel and skinned shins were commonplace.

The wheel, about six feet in diameter, was cylindrical in shape and worked like a revolving drum. This drum would have about twenty treadboards, be up to eighty feet long but divided into four sections, each section taking eight men. Prisoners would mount a standing platform board before stepping upon it. Each prisoner was screened from the next making communication impossible. The treadwheel operated a shaft which in turn operated a series of intermeshing cog wheels which turned the grindstones over the corn. The cornmill ground enough flour to supply the gaol inmates plus some of the four hundred inmates in the County Asylm, and the bran left over was sold to the public.

In 1827 in the old gaol a prisoner named Sowden refused to work the wheel. Fellow inmates followed his example and a riot ensued. Despite the Cornish Militia restoring general order Sowden stood his ground. He was eventually flogged with the cat-of-nine tails into submission and took his turn on the wheel. In 1823, Sir Robert Peel's Act emphasised '*prevention and deterrence based on a disciplinary system*'. Stories about the treadwheel would certainly have proved a deterrent. At one time a handmill was also in use but because it took so much longer to grind the grain using this method as opposed to the treadwheel, it was soon discontinued.

Flogging scene.

Oakum picking.
Prisoners were expected to produce over 41/2 lbs of fibre per day.

OAKUM PICKING:
Oakum is defined in the dictionary as a 'caulking fibre got by picking old rope to pieces'. The old rope would have mainly come from the dockyards. It was cut into two of three feet lengths and given to the prisoners to work on in their cells. They would beat the rope against a block of wood until the strands separated. The prisoners would pick at these strands and turn them into small fibres. The end product was oakum. The oakum was then sent back to the shipyards to be mixed with tar. This product was caulking fibre and was used between the wooden seams of ships' deck planking. Oakum was also used in mat making and stuffing mattresses. Female prisoners sentenced to hard labour would also have been given oakum picking. It was very painful work, for the fingers became red raw and would bleed with the continual picking. The prison would make up to £100 per year profit by selling the oakum.

The following is a copy of the prison regulations given to each prisoner on his admittance to Bodmin gaol:

ABSTRACT OF THE REGULATIONS

RELATING TO THE

TREATMENT AND CONDUCT

OF

CONVICTED PRISONERS

1. Prisoners shall preserve silence.

2. They shall not communicate, or attempt to do so, with one another, or with any strangers or others who may visit the Prison.

3. They shall keep themselves clean and decent in their persons and shall obey such regulations as regards washing, bathing, and in the case of male prisoners, hair-cutting, as may from time to time be established, with a view to the proper maintenance of health and cleanliness.

4. They shall keep their cells, utensils, clothing, and bedding, clean and neatly arranged; and shall, when required, clean and sweep the yards, passages, and other parts of the prison.

5. If any prisoner has any complaint to make regarding the diet, it must be made immediately after a meal is served. Frivolous and groundless complaints, repeatedly made, will be dealt with a breach of Prison discipline.

6. A prisoner may if required for purposes of justice, be photographed and measured on reception and subsequently.

7. A prisoner committed to Prison for non-payment of a sum adjudged to be paid *by the conviction* of any court of summary jurisdiction, may obtain a reduction of a part of the sentence by paying part of the sum for which he is liable, viz., the fine, costs, and cost of commitment. No such payment shall be made on Sunday, or on a week-day before 9a .m.

8. Prisoners shall attend Divine Service on Sundays and on other days when such Service is performed, unless they receive permission to be absent. Prisoners shall not be compelled to attend the religious service of a Church to which they do not belong.

9. If any Prisoner who is of a religious persuasion different from that of the Established Church specially so requests, the Governor shall permit a minister of that persuasion to visit him at proper and reasonable times under regulations approved by the Commissioners.

10. The following offences committed by prisoners will render them liable to punishment:—

1. Disobeying any order of the Governor or of any other officer, or any Prison regulation.

2. Treating with disrespect any officer or servant of the Prison, or any visitor, or any person employed in connection with the Prison or works.

3. Being idle, careless, or negligent at work, or refusing to work.

4. Being absent without leave from Divine Service, or prayers, or school instruction.

5. Behaving irreverently at Divine Service of prayers.

6. Swearing, cursing, or using any abusive, insolent, threatening, or other improper language.

7. Being indecent in language, act, or gesture.

8. Committing a common assault upon another prisoner.

9. Conversing or holding intercourse with another prisoner without authority.

10. Singing, whistling, or making any unnecessary noise, or giving any unnecessary trouble.

11. Leaving his cell or other appointed location, or his place or work, without permission.

12. In any way disfiguring or damaging any part of the Prison, or any article to which he may have access.

13. Committing any nuisance.

14. Having in his cell or possession any article he is not allowed to have.

15. Giving to or receiving from any prisoner any article whatever without leave.

16. In any other way offending against good order and discipline.

17. Attempting to do any of the foregoing things.

18. Personal violence to a fellow prisoner.

19. Grossly offensive or abusive language to any officer or servant of the Prison.

20. Wilfully or wantonly breaking the Prison windows, or otherwise destroying the Prison property.

21. When under punishment, wilfully making a disturbance tending to interrupt the order and discipline of the Prison.

22. Any other act of gross misconduct or insubordination requiring to be suppressed by extraordinary means.

23. Escaping or attempting to escape from Prison.

11. The following offences committed by male prisoners will render them liable to corporal punishment:—

1. Mutiny or incitement to munity.

2. Gross personal violence to any officer or servant of the Prison.

12. Prisoners may, if they desire, have an interview with the Governor or Superior Authority, to make complaints or prefer requests; and the Governor shall redress any grievance or take such steps as may seem necessary.

13. Any prisoner wishing to see a member of the Visiting Committee shall be allowed to do so on the occasion of his next occurring visit to the Prison.

Punishments handed out to prisoners for failing to adhere to this Charter of Prison Regulations would have included being placed in irons, sent to confinement in a permanently dark cell, having their diet stopped or reduced, and in extreme cases transportation.

After receiving this sheet of prison regulations each prisoner would be escorted to a reception cell where he/she would undergo a medical examination to assess their fitness for their proposed work programme. They would be issued prison clothing and given a bath.

Prison shirts were made of cotton or flannel, or a smock-style without buttons. Prison-made leather slippers were provided. The colour of the prisoners' clothing varied according to the crime committed and was loosely linked to the class section mentioned earlier. Minor offenders wore grey for men, blue for women; those gaoled for felony, a crime deemed to be graver than a misdemeanour, wore red and grey broad stripes for men, blue and white for women; men not sentenced to hard labour wore black and yellow check. Stockings and caps were worn showing their appropriate corridor/gallery marking. Shirts and jackets were marked with the prisoner's cell number enabling the warders to identify each prisoner at a glance. One can imagine the confusion in the changing rooms if Bodmin gaol had ever raised a football team! During inclement weather thick warm capes were issued for wearing while exercising outdoors. If the weather became too foul then exercise was taken indoors.

Compared to the living conditions of the old gaol, the new gaol

BODMIN GAOL 1860.

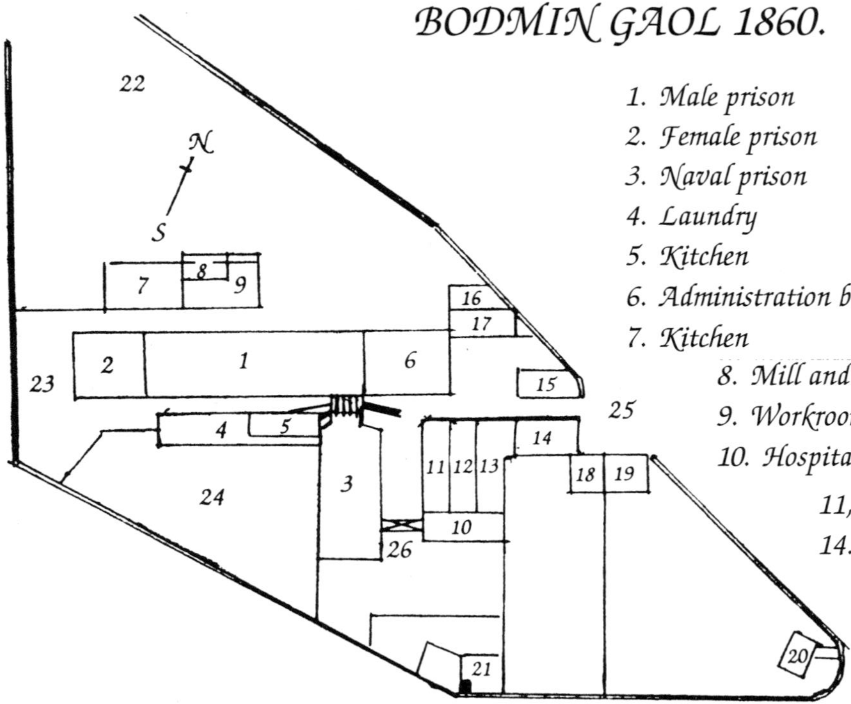

1. *Male prison*
2. *Female prison*
3. *Naval prison*
4. *Laundry*
5. *Kitchen*
6. *Administration block, library, chapel above*
7. *Kitchen*
8. *Mill and treadwheel*
9. *Workroom*
10. *Hospital*

11, 12, 13, *Offices & store*
14. *Porter's lodge*
15. *Quarters*
16. *Stabling*
17. *Hay/Straw Barn*
18. *Governor's house*
19. *Chaplaincy*
20. *Governor's/Chaplain's stables*
21. *Officer's quarters*
22. *Gardens*
23. *Female exercise yard*
24. *Main exercise yard*
25. *Main entrance*
26. *Passageway between cellblock & hospital*

BODMIN GAOL TODAY

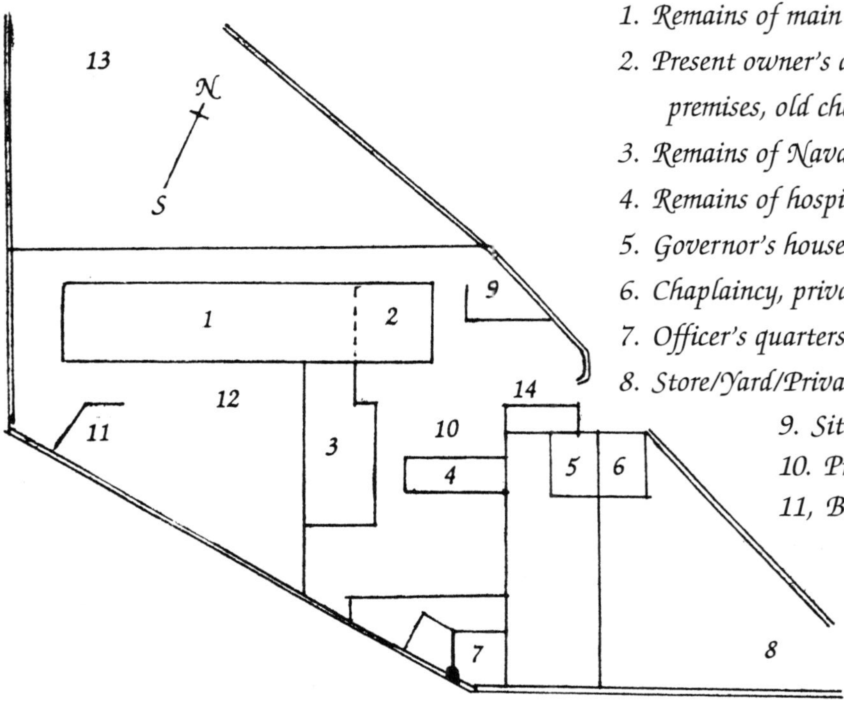

1. Remains of main block
2. Present owner's accommodation, licenced premises, old chapel above
3. Remains of Naval prison
4. Remains of hospital
5. Governor's house, privately owned
6. Chaplaincy, privately owned
7. Officer's quarters, privatelyt owned
8. Store/Yard/Private accommodation
9. Site of execution shed
10. Present day workshop
11, Builder's shop
12. Builder's yard with planning permission for industrial units
13. Housing estate
14. Visitor's entrance

offered prisoners vast improvements. Each prisoner now received clean sheets and a pillow as well as blankets. Cells contained a jug of fresh water, washing bowl, slop pot, and materials to ensure clean implements and a clean cell.

Basic cell implements plus prayer book, Bible and hymn book.

At the Chaplain's discretion prisoners were allowed a Bible, a prayer book and a hymn book. The Chaplain would also assess the prisoner's level of intelligence. If below average they would be given two hours schooling per week on the basics of reading and writing. Some were regarded as hopeless cases and left alone, while those inmates over forty years of age were deemed not worth persevering with.

PRIVILEGES:

The new gaol contained a library, but before prisoners were allowed to use it they had to earn the right. The library, further education, the writing and receiving of letters, and visitors, were all regarded as privileges. Each privilege had to be earned with a number of marks or points. These marks were accumulated in stages, each stage representing 224 marks. A maximum of 56 marks could be earned in any one day.

Stage 1 allowed the prisoner books on religious instruction and education.

Stage 2 allowed the prisoner books on religious instruction and education, plus one library book per week and additional school instruction.

Stage 3 allowed the prisoner the privileges of stage two plus one extra library book per week, permission to write and receive one letter, and permission to receive one visit of twenty minutes.

Stage 4 allowed the prisoner the privileges of stage three with visitors allowed an extra ten minutes, and additional visitors for gaining just another 112 marks.

As each privilege was taken the appropriate number of marks were deducted from the prisoner's score card and more marks had to be earned before the privileges were granted again. This marking and stage system was in use around the end of the nineteenth century and start of the twentieth century. As with the class system re length of sentence determining prisoners' diets, this marking and scoring of points seems rather complicated. Perhaps records were kept on some sort of nineteenth century calculator. Presumably the marks were won by the prisoner's good behaviour and profitable labour output. A few prisoners earned the star privilege of being allowed to hold conversation with a fellow prisoner for one hour per week. A strict code of silence was enforced at all other times.

As the gaol progressed towards the twentieth century conditions and regulations moved with the times. Labour practises were revised and before the turn of the century the treadwheel was abolished. The number of hours prisoners were expected to work became less, and more variation was introduced to the working day. Oakum picking remained, coal bag making and mail bag sewing were introduced. More prisoners were allocated work in the gaol's gardens. A lot of the canvass goods were sold to our Forces during the Boer War (1899-1902), contributing to the overall profit of £1,000 the prison is recorded as having made in 1901. Many of the coal bags were used by the Royal Navy on the steam-powered warships. Bag making was accomplished in the prisoner's cell,

System of Association Labour. Groups of prisoners working together but in strict silence.

but after a month of working alone they qualified for the 'System of Association Labour'. This reform, introduced in 1902, involved groups of up to twenty prisoners working together. However, the work was still conducted in absolute silence.

Female prisoners working in gaol laundry. Each prisoner worked in her own cubicle again in strict silence.

Female prisoners worked mainly in the laundry.

This adjoined the kitchens and was south of the main male cell block. It was screened from the exercise yard. It occupied a ground floor area of nearly eighty square yards.

Each prisoner entered a cubicle fitted with washing and rinsing sinks and its own water supply. The cubicle door was locked and again all work conducted in silence. A wardress was always in attendance to ensure a ready supply of dirty linen and to receive the clean. Mr. Fred Hellen recalls the prison's water supply rises near Fairwash, Lower Whitley, and runs down the valley, past Cuckoo Quarry and Flaxmoor Terrace, then disappears under Bodiniel Road. It runs under the prison and emerges again alongside the Camel Trail and eventually reaches the River Camel. The laundry and kitchens have since been demolished.

Female offenders at exercise.

There were three exercise yards, probably two for male prisoners and one for the women. Exercise was not compulsory, usually followed breakfast, and was for a duration of up to an hour. Whilst at exercise the women prisoners were compelled to wear large bonnet-style hats to prevent visual as well as oral communication. One sees similar fashions today at Royal Ascot!

Chapel interior.

Exercise was followed by a chapel service. The original chapel windors can still be seen today although the inside no longer resembles its former purpose.

In 1911 the women's section of the gaol was closed, Plymouth receiving female offenders after this date. Bodmin gaol has seen its fair share of 'real hard cases' among the female inmates. Between 1870 - 1871 three were placed in irons, seventeen had their diet reduced, and a further eighteen sent to the dark cell - all for breaking prison regulations. One governor is quoted as saying "we have had women we could not tame, but never a man". Nothing much changes!

The Naval Prison

Imprisonment for juvenile offenders had been discontinued and the Debtors Act of 1869 saw a demise in prison sentencing for debt. This enabled the Admiralty to take over part of the civil prison and transfer naval prisoners to Bodmin. The new gaol had received the odd naval offender but in 1887 a complete wing was transferred to their management. Prior to this naval prisoners were detained in Devonport Gaol. In 1892 two houses adjoining the gateway in the south wall were built for naval officials. These are now privately owned. The first Governor of the Naval Prison was Captain Malcolm McNeile. He was succeeded by Captain G.S. McIlwaine who in turn was succeeded by M.B. Cartwright.

The Naval Block. After some alterations this wing of the civil prison was transferred to the naval authorities in 1887. All that remains today are the four walls and ground floor cells.

In 1910 Commander Thomas Brandreth was appointed Naval Governor and he held the post until the closure of the naval prison in 1922.

Following alterations in 1901, the naval prison contained one hundred and five cells on four floor levels. The main walls and ground floor cells remain intact today and can still be viewed. Also visible from the south entrance of the remains of the naval block are the landing's support spurs and internal granite staircase.

In 1905 the chief warder of the naval prison was Mr. J. Edmunds who had come to Bodmin in 1887 and held prior positions in the prison of clerk and storekeeper.

The naval block was connected to the hospital by an enclosed passageway at first floor level. The sealed ends of this passageway are visible today but most of the hospital has been reduced to rubble. In 1919 several British seamen found guilty of offences in Northern Russia were sent to Bodmin to serve between three and five years imprisonment. Due to increasing costs the Admiralty closed the naval prison in 1922.

Bodmin was the last naval prison in this country.

Quarters for naval officers, now privately owned.

Final Years

Between 1800 - 1860 Cornwall's population increased considerably but towards the end of the nineteenth century the growth rate had slowed and by the turn of the century was actually in decline. This was largely due to the demise of the mining industry. Copper

Many examples of old mine workings can be found throughout Cornwall. The area around St. Just and Botallack in particular is rich in mining history.

mining had peaked in 1856 and yet by 1890 had virtually collapsed, output below that of 1780. Tin mining was also in decline and the china clay industry was too young to offer sufficient alternative labour opportunities.

For many Cornish miners and dependents of the mining industry emigration offered a better lifestyle. North and South America, South Africa and Australia drew many immigrant Cornish miners. Free passages to South Australia for suitable tradesmen were advertised in the Cornish press. This decline in population contributed to the decrease in the number of offenders being sent to gaol and a Prison Commissioner's report of 1909 concluded the majority of prisoners were vagrants. People were imprisoned for begging, and having no place of residence, and then released after a few days, only to be taken in again the next week. In 1916 the prison authorities decided to close the civil prison. The last Governor was H.L. Browett who had presumably succeeded Mr. Shenton. Future offenders committed to gaol were sent to either Plymouth or Exeter. The naval prison continued in use until 1922 and in 1927 the whole gaol was formally closed.

The civil prison was closed during the First World War and Bodmin gaol was entrusted with the safekeeping of some of the nation's treasures. Records show that State Papers and the Domesday book were among treasures sent to Bodmin from the Public Record Office in London. Several of the local folk would also say that the Crown Jewels were included in these treasures.

Shepton Mallet gaol in Somerset housed the same items during the Second World War.

1929 - 1990

At 3.00 p.m. on February 7th, 1929 at the Royal Hotel, Bodmin, the prison, staff and officers' quarters, Governor's House and Chaplaincy, and gardens, were all put up for auction. Messrs. D. Ward and Son of Plymouth conducted the proceedings.

The civil prison was sold for £1,050 to Mr. T.S. Lee of Ipswich who intended to demolish the gaol and sell the materials to various contractors and then make subsequent use of the site. The quarters now known as Flaxmoor Terrace were sold individually and fetched between £200 and £300 each. The gardens were sold in various lots and raised around £80 in total. The purchaser of the Governor's House and Chaplaincy was Mr. George Hellen who paid £600 for each property - George Hellen being the father of Fred Hellen mentioned earlier in this book.

Lee removed the rooves for the slates and lead, but when he came to demolish the walls found that the granite refused to break down into uniform sized blocks but shattered into many shapes and sizes. This was due to the original building adhesives of limestone rather than mortar. The limestone had fused with the granite. Mr. Fred Hellen recalls dynamite being used in the attempted demolition.

For a while the prison was opened as a tourist attraction; although the numbers of visitors to the West Country were only a fraction of what they are today, tourism was beginning to benefit the local economy. Previous gaol warders were employed as prison guides. However, this business venture did not last very long and the gaol was sold again. Local businessman, George Smith, whose son Ronald runs a furniture store in Bodmin, purchased the gaol and used it as a base for his haulage contracting business. The naval block was also purchased.

Subsequent owners were a Mr. and Mrs. Dobell who opened a nightclub on the premises, Mr. Smith again, a Mr. Allen, Mr. G. Morecombe, Mr. Mason and the present owner, Mr. Terry Gilhooly. Mr. Gilhooly opens part of the gaol to visitors during the holiday season and also runs a bar and restaurant on the premises.

The gardens previously behind the main civil prison have been developed into a housing estate, although the outer prison wall remain virtually intact. The south wall remains and the main exercise yard is at present owned and used by a local building firm. Although offering fine views of the old civil prison block and naval block, with their cell windows and bars still intact, it is not open to the public.

HANGINGS
~ LIST OF EXECUTIONS AT BODMIN ~

On Bodmin Moor:

1785	March 7th	Philip Randal	aged 21	Burglary
1785	March 23	Robert Brown	aged 33	Murder
1785	July 29th	William Hill	aged 25	Murder
1785	August 7th	John Richards	aged 25	Robbery with violence
1786	April 6th	Thomas Roberts	aged 34	Steeling three sheep
1786	April 26th	Francis Couth	aged 45	Stealing a ewe
1787	April 10th	James Elliott	aged 35	Highway robbery
1787	April 10th	John Gould	aged 23	Burglary
1787	August 20th	William Congdon	aged 22	Stealing a watch
1791	March 31st	Michael Taylor	aged 22	Stealing a mare
1791	March 31st	John Dash	aged 23	Burglary
1791	March 31st	James Symons	aged 25	Stealing an ox
1791	Sept. 2nd	Ben Willoughby	aged 20	Murder
1791	Sept. 2nd	John Taylor	aged 26	Murder
1791	Sept. 15th	William Moyle	-	Killing a mare
1795	April 9th	James Frederick	aged 33	Robbery

1795	August 27th	Joseph Williams	aged 28	Stealing a sheep
1796	-	G.A. Safehorne	-	Murder
1796	August 11th	John Hoskin	aged 55	Stealing wheat
1798	Sept. 13th	William Howarth	aged 24	Stealing
1801	April 13th	William Roskilly	aged 34	Housebreaking
1802	August 25th	Richard Andrew	-	Forgery

On Bodmin Moor or outside the wall of the old gaol:

1802	Sept. 2nd	John Vanstone	aged 37	Robbery
1802	Sept. 2nd	William Lee	-	Robbery
1805	April 17th	John Williamson	aged 32	Shopbreaking
1805	April 17th	James Joyce	aged 27	Shopbreaking
1812	April 13th	Pierrre Francois	aged 24	Forgery
1812	May 1st	William Wyatt	aged 40	Murder
1813	Sept. 6th	Elizabeth Osbourne	aged 20	Arson
1814	March 31st	William Burns	aged 21	Murder
1815	March 31st	John Simms	aged 30	Murder

Public hangings outside the wall of the old gaol:

1820	August 12th	Sarah Polgreen	aged 37	Poisoning her husband
1820	Sept. 5th	Michael Stephens	aged 27	Killing a ram
1821	April 2nd	John Barnicott	aged 24	Murder
1821	April 2nd	John Thompson	aged 17	Murder
1821	Sept. 10th	Nicholas Good	aged 42	Murder
1825	April 7th	William Oxford	aged 21	Arson
1827	April 19th	James Eddy	aged 29	Highway robbery
1828	August 8th	Elizabeth Commins	aged 22	Murder
1828	August 21st	Thomas Coombe	aged 21	Housebreaking
1834	August 21st	William Hocking	aged 57	Bestiality
1835	March 30th	John Henwood	aged 29	Murder
1840	April 13th	William Lightfoot	aged 36	Murder

1840	April 13th	James Lightfoot	aged 23	Murder
1844	August 12th	Matthew Weeks	aged 24	Murder
1845	August 11th	Ben Ellison	aged 61	Murder
1854	April 3rd	James Holman	aged 27	Murder of wife
1856	August 11th	William Nevin	aged 44	Murder

New gaol:

1862	August 18th	John Doidge	aged 28	Murder

Executed inside the new gaol but not viewed by the public:

1878	August 15th	Selina Wadge	aged 29	Murder
1882	Nov. 13th	William Bartlett	aged 46	Murder

Executed inside the new gaol on thet new site known as the execution shed and not viewed by the public:

1901	July 9th	Giovanni Valeri	aged 31	Murder at sea
1909	July 20th	William Hampton	aged 24	Murder

On April 10th, 1787, James Elliott of Padstow was hanged for being found guilty of highway robbery. Elliott had been baptised in the font of St. Petroc's Church, Padstow, and superstition was that anyone baptised there would never go to the gallows. Being found guilty was a great surprise to many locals, but when Elliott died on the gallows the superstition died also.

Two more superstitions survived much longer, both concerning the hangman's rope. It was custom to sell the rope after a hanging. It would be cut into many small lengths and sold for a shilling a time. When worn round the neck it was thought to cure any number of ailments, and also direct the wearer on a straight and Godly path.

In 1813 Elizabeth Osbourne was hanged for setting fire to a cornstack. This was held to be a very serious crime for there was an acute shortage of corn. The previous year had seen rioting in the streets by Cornish miners complaining of the high prices being charged by corn merchants.

The Lightfoot Brothers

On Monday, April 13th, 1840 William and James Lightfoot were executed for the murder of a thirty-eight year-old local man, Nevell Norway. The Lightfoot brothers lived near Wadebridge and had acquired a reputation for being a troublesome pair. On the night of February 8th, 1840 they lay in wait for a wealthy miller on his way home from Bodmin market, intending to rob him. Nevell Norway, a much respected tradesman who had even been charitable to the Lightfoots in the past, happened to pass their way before the intended victim.

They attacked him, knocked him off his horse and clubbed him to death. His body was found the next morning laying in a ditch after a search was organised by a farmer who had discovered his horse saddled and tacked up, wandering and grazing the grass verges.

For a while, despite a detective from London handling the murder enquiry, no suspicion could be levelled at anyone. Bodmin Town Council offered a reward for information. Persistent investigation found a local man who recalled seeing the Lightfoots in the vicinity on the night of the murder. Also, a neighbour of one of the Lightfoot brothers remembered hearing Lightfoot comforting his wife who was crying and weeping on the same night in question, and then a few days later hearing both the Lighfoot wives arguing. One was heard to say, "Your man killed Mr. Norway", the other wife retorted, "No, it was your man". William and James Lightfoot were arrested and after being held in custody for a few days admitted to the murder. They were tried on March 30th, 1840, found guilty and sentenced to hang. News of the impending hangings spread throughout Cornwall, and the local railway company ran special trains from Wadebridge to Bodmin to accommodate the sightseers. The railway's spur line from Boscarne Junction to Bodmin North ran alongside the prison's south wall and provided perfect viewing facilities. Estimates of the number of spectators varied. The 'West Briton' newspaper put the figure at 25,000: another bumper pay day for Bodmin tradesmen! An appeal set up to provide financial support for Mrs. Norway and her six children raised in excess of £3,500, a truly vast sum of money for that period of time.

Nevell Norway is buried in Egloshayle churchyard. The grave's headstone confirms the date and manner of Norway's death, and to the sum of money contributed to the fund set up to support his family.

Egloshayle is situated on the north side of the River Camel, nearly opposite Wadebridge. The two communities were joined in September 1991 by the erection of a footbridge over the river thanks to the B.B.C. Television programme "Challenge Anneka".

Escapes

Both the old and the new gaols were reasonably secure, Once a prisoner was locked in their cell the only way out was through the door. However, records show at least ten escapes occurred between 1812 - 1833. Most of these were probably achieved by means of bribery.

Some prisoners attempted to scale the prison wall but the drop on the other side was considerable. Mr. Jack Gough, a Bodmin man, and one of the partners in the building firm at present occupying the main exercise yard inside the south wall, recalls as a boy a story of a prisoner who, having scaled the south wall, dropped over the other side. His body was found the next day near Scarlett's Well. He had apparaently crawled to the well having suffered multiple injuries as a result of his leap to freedom. There is supposedly an arrow on the wall marking the spot where the prisoner escaped, but over the years it has either weathered away or become overgrown with bracken, for there is no sign of it today.

A mass escape was attempted in 1832 whilst the prison governor and some gaolers were attending Quarter Sessions in Truro. Their effort was contained by the remaining staff and other prisoners.

One December night in 1833 several escapees were recaptured on Bodmin Moor suffering from exposure. The Moor is not the best place to be if lightly clothed on a Summer's night, lef alone on a night in the middle of Winter. George Kendall and John Bayley escaped during August 1812. Despite a reward being offered for their recapture the escape was apparently successful. How they escaped records do not explain.

John Bull's famous Cornish Inn;

or,

Bodmin Jail, both out and in.

In Bodmin's pretty country town—
Though not a place of great renown—
There is a spot remembered well,
Where stands Bull's famous branch hotel.

Wheel and oakum, tread and tease,
So wearisome and slow ;
Crank and jobbing, turn and grease,
And round the ring they go.

Regardless of expense 'twas built,
Outside there's neither show nor gilt ;
But if you go you'll get a cell,
At John Bull's famous branch hotel.

Blue dress for those who are untried,
And brown for those who have been tried ;
But in these togs they look queer coves,
Just like pork hams stuck o'er with cloves.

A pris'ner's life's a dreary one,
No talk, nor knocking to and fro ;
And while at Bull's all sport is done
At theatre, market, fair or show.

All things are bleak at that hotel,
And not for you my honest swell ;
But he who's morally impure
May be turned out a perfect cure.

The doctor tries to keep them whole ;
The earnest parson strives to sow
The Word into each darkened soul
Though seldom grows a holy glow.

The morning service in the hall
Have sacred charms for one and all ;
The Sunday rest they pleasant find,
With sound-sense books to store the mind.

The breakfasts, suppers, are quite light,
With Adam's ale they can't get tight ;
The bill of fare's not fare for Bill,
Who likes his pipe and loves his gill.

For victuals they've variety—
Brown bread of ... quality,
Porridge, gruel and stirabout ;
Six months cures corpulence and gout.

They've also bacon, beans and beef—
Too good, you say, for rogue or thief—
Soup, cocoa, spuds and suet duff ;
But here's the pinch—there's ne'er enough.

An ounce of bacon once a week,
Make many play at hide and seek ;
The half-pint soup goes quickly o'er—
In vain the dish is licked for more.

Tin washing basin, plate and pan,
Tin mug, meat dishes, water can ;
Comb, brush and soap, salt-box and spoon,
And prayers hung up for morn and noon.

But there are neither knives nor forks,
Though plenty screws but not for corks ;
Bracelets, but not for ladies' wrists,
Badges, but not for honest breasts.

"System of progressive stages,"
Mean a scale of marks and wages ;
For first month there is no reward :
The next a bob without the "hard."

The other two are really bricks,
For both combin'd bring three and six ;
Though if they one or two stretch did,
There's nothing more than half a quid.

The nightly movements on the plank
Are something sim'lar to the crank ;
It's round and round from night till morn,
And glad to rise, though sore and worn.

The treadwheel's spirit-breaking task,
Like night-mare in a half-closed cask ;
Or pickles, sweets, dessert and cake,
When jaws and ev'ry tooth does ache.

For breach of rules—handcuffs behind,
Belt, birch, eight inches, dark confined ;
The penal pound, with Adam's wine,
The canvas dress, the cat-o'-nine.

When on triangles, getting bashed,
Which means tied up and being lashed,
They think—while screws are taking chops—
Of glass, and pipe, and fancy shops.

Those dear, familiar sounds we hear—
The crow of cock and caw of crow—
Mind of sweet liberty so near
To that grim den of silent woe.

The worst's the pack of wolfish screws,
Whose looks do out, whose words do bruise ;
Though flesh breaks down, with hard, rough fare :
The wounded spirit's worst to bear.

Those who have been to that famed place
May know to some there's no disgrace ;
For there are some who get a trip
To Bull's hotel for giving lip.

Take this advice before we part—
Be thou a stranger, friend or foe—
Do what is right, where'er thou art,
Lest Cornwall County Jail you know.

PETER S. SINCLAIR.